How to Draw Cool and Simple Things

By Amy Hughes

Table of Contents

Disclaimer

While all attempts have been made to verify the information provided in this book, the author does assume any responsibility for errors, omissions, or contrary interpretations of the subject matter contained within. **The information provided in this book is for educational and entertainment purposes only. The reader is responsible for his or her own actions and the author does not accept any responsibilities for any liabilities or damages, real or perceived, resulting from the use of this information.**

The trademarks that are used are without any consent, and the publication of the trademark is without permission or backing by the trademark owner. All trademarks and brands within this book are for clarifying purposes only and are the owned by the owners themselves, not affiliated with this document.

Introduction

I want to thank you and congratulate you for downloading the book, "Drawing for Beginners".

This book contains proven steps and strategies on how to sketch.

To start, an aide on the best way to draw ought to exhibit a decent comprehension of the difficulties that outline craftsmen face.

As in any business you go over, some much of the time made inquiries will rise with time. The inquiry is, has the creator set aside the time to tissue out these FAQs? What's more, has the writer set aside the time to take a seat and truly think about the answers before offering them to the peruser?

These central comprehensions of the difficulties shape the fundamental system for any great sketching aide. Be that as it may, even with this system, the peruser needs to know whether the creator has the capacity answer the inquiries precisely and give sound arrangements that work.

Case in point, numerous individuals on my site has discovered drawing pictures troublesome. This can be further separated to the diverse elements on a face. Some discover drawing noses extreme, while others discover drawing lips dubious. I've additionally understood that numerous craftsmen have an issue with getting extents right.

They have this picture they need to attract their psyche yet when they put it down on paper, it some way or another turns out off-base. So how would we start to address this?

Characterizing the issue precisely is just the first step. Presently the arrangements should be introduced plainly. For example, to take care of the issue of getting extents right, one ought to have a framework for estimation.

Estimation is everything in extents. Specialists misunderstand extents on the grounds that as people, we don't generally draw what we see. Have a go at drawing a circle and you'll comprehend what I mean. To compound the situation, our feeling of relativity is likewise incorrect. As it were, the point at which we attract something that is connection to something else, we quite often get the estimations off-base. The trap to defeat this is not to put an excessive amount of trust on our freehand capacities and rely on upon a framework for precise estimations.

In the event that you can build up that the creator of the sketching aide has possessed the capacity to express the difficulties and arrangements obviously, you know you're in for a treat.

Sketching is the expertise of reproducing any perspective on paper with only a couple strokes in no time flat. Anybody can figure out how to draw with some fundamental perception aptitudes. This potential is open at any age!

As a pastime, pencil sketching offers a distinct option for putting your considerations onto paper when words are insufficient to do as such. It is shoddy; everything you need is a pencil and a bit of paper. It is conceivable to portray anyplace, at whatever time. In the event that you decide to do as such, you can offer your fine art.

This instructional exercise is gotten from mulling over old craftsmanship books composed long prior and shares all significant data which can be viewed as the legacy left by incredible craftsmen of more seasoned times. All the regulated guidelines have been consolidated into one downloadable pdf and in this way sparing you hours of exploration from various books. You will discover all that you have to learn.

There are various approaches to make portrays. Beginning from the rudiments, this eBook makes figuring out how to outline so snappy and simple. The straightforward illustrations and tips makes how to draw eBook so natural to peruse and get it. You will discover a great deal of accommodating tips, activities and uplifting statements which creates certainty and consolation to its peruser.

It's understood that individuals learn best by seeing and doing. You will learn precisely the same route in this instructional exercise guide. In different universes you will learn by sketching more quickly than by whatever other means consolidated. You should simply rehearse the activities given in instructional exercise direct so you can comprehend the procedure better. With the assistance of the instructional exercises you will learn tips for: having a decent begin which heading strokes ought to take after for diverse articles. utilizing strokes to represent surface masterminding strokes for impact

The lessons are conveyed immediately in pdf design. This organization gives this aide another favorable position in light of the fact that the moment conveyance on the web spares you time and cash. There is no bundling and transportation to pay for and no holding up time. It is conceivable to peruse the material inside this book directly after the buy.

Learning Event 1:

Distinguish AND DESCRIBE THE TOOLS USED TO APPLY, REMOVE, OR AFFIX THE IMAGE TO THE DRAWING SURFACE

1. Devices are utilized to apply, uproot, or fasten the medium to the drawing surface. A device can join the medium like graphite in a pencil.

This image shows you how to start the work of drawing the jar, the lines are for general sketch so that your drawing is symmetrical.

   a. Pencils, the most generally utilized, minimum lavish drawing instruments, are really the packaging encompassing a medium. Charcoal, carbon, and graphite are the most widely recognized sorts of pencils utilized as a part of practical drawing.

(1) Charcoal comes in five evaluations and can be in stick or pencil structure. It delivers a dull, thick dark line. These pencils come in six evaluations from 10B (delicate) to HH (medium hard).
(2) Graphite (erroneously alluded to as lead) pencils are reviewed by hardness

Lead is a delicate, exceptionally sparkly metal. Lead pencils are uncommon today, and have been supplanted by graphite.

As now you can see the jug is symmetrical

(a) Hardness evaluations are imprinted on the pencils, e.g., a delicate graphite pencil is the 6B which delivers the darkest, boldest line. The hardest is the 9H which creates a lighter line. Be cautious when attempting to make lighter tones with a delicate pencil. You may make an undesirable grainy impact. On the other hand, you can exploit a textured impact in the event that you require it.

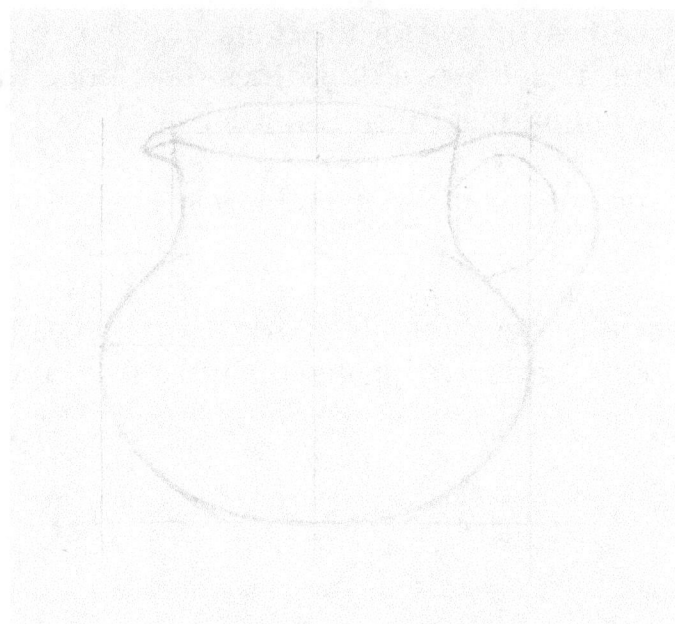

Now you can see as the image shows the sketch is proper in dimensions and looks fine

(b) Carpenter's pencils (rectangular graphite) are utilized for enhancements applications, for example, drawing shingles, leaf examples, and different subjects. See on how to hone and hold a woodworker's pencil, and an illustration of an enhancement application.

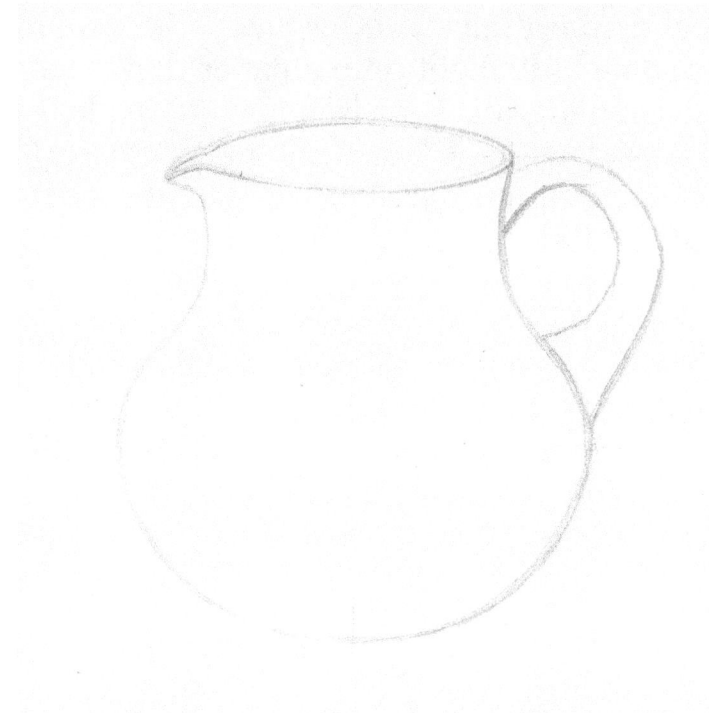

Now you can erase all the lines which you made in the 1st figure and the jug is ready.

Gear

The most troublesome errand in creating an exact attracting is to place every one of the parts of the subject in the opportune spot, whilst guaranteeing that they are of the right extent to different parts of the same drawing what's more, to the same scale. To accomplish this, the most helpful bit of gear is a Camera which is all the more precisely depicted as a Tracing Device. All the top magnifying lens producers create such a gadget to be utilized with their own magnifying instruments yet they are extremely extravagant when purchased new. I have utilized two distinct sorts.

The main is an extraordinary x10 eyepiece with an inner crystal, which diverts some of its light onto a paper that is set before the magnifying instrument, this runs well magnifying lens then again other more seasoned metal sorts intended to work with any compound magnifying instrument. These are now and then acessible second hand.

The second choice is a mirror arm and crystal, which fits numerous magnifying lens' eyepiece or are currently planned by cutting edge makers to be put between the destinations and eyepiece on a secluded plan. This sort additionally functions admirably with stereo magnifying instruments.

Figure 1:

(a)Originally, specialized wellspring pens were utilized for decision straight uniform lines in drafting. They are likewise suited to freehand drawings.

These pens include an ink supply appended to the barrel of the pen. A few repositories are translucent plastic cartridges inside of the body of the pen. Ink is conveyed to the surface through an empty shaft of a food tube which frames the point. Ink stream is controlled by the cleaning pin what's more, gravity. The expansive ink supply held by the cartridge decreases ink stacking time and the possibility of a spill. In the wake of utilizing the pens, wash all parts in running water and blotch dry. In the event that ink dries in the pens, absorb them pen-cleaning arrangement and clean them completely.

(b)   Ballpoint pens are like wellspring pens. The ink is moved on by a little ball situated at the tip of the supply. The ink supply and point are for all time joined.

(c)

At the point when the ink is gone, toss out and supplant the pen. Ballpoint pens now and again oblige a wipe of the tip, generally there is no cleaning. They come in sizes from expansive to additional fine.

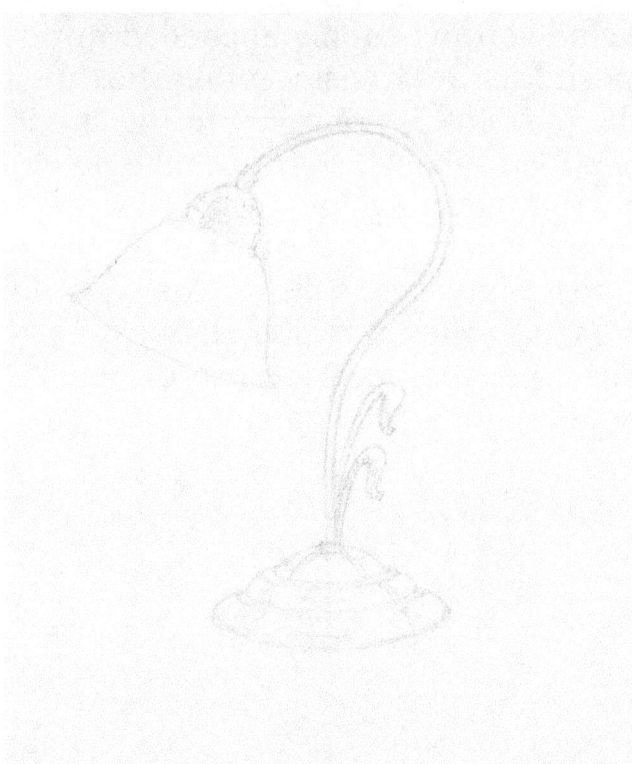

(d)   Felt-tip pens and markers have a nylon or felt center that appropriates ink to the focuses. The purpose of felt tips, similar to ballpoints, is for all time joined to the ink supply. Toss the apparatus away when the ink supply is depleted. These pens arrive in a vast mixed bag of diverse point sizes and shapes. The ink in most felt tips is waterproof and dries right away.

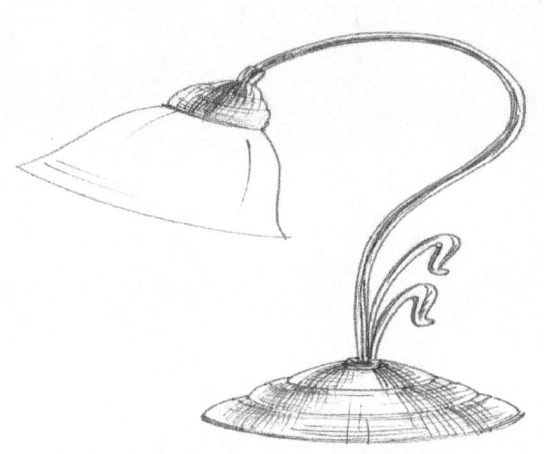

b. Use brushes to apply most fluid media to a surface. The style of drawing, the medium utilized, and the system needed will focus the brush sort you will utilize. The three most regular brushes are the round, level, and splendid.

(1) Round brushes come to focuses which fluctuate from sharp to limit. Utilization properly measured rounds to apply or skim on washes.

(2) Flat brushes have straight edges and expansive tips. The straightened ferrule gives these brushes their shape. Pads ought to be around 2 1/2 times longer than they are wide. Utilize a substantial level (1 to 3-inch firm swarmed) house paint brush for mixing huge ranges of solid tone or shading media. Moreover, there are extraordinary utilization brushes, e.g., a fan brush for including composition.

(3) Brights are shorter than level brushes in that they are just around 1/2 times as long as they are wide. Brights

have genuinely sharp corners. Brights perform well for applying a thick, solid medium.

1. The surface to which you apply media is of real significance. The most widely recognized surfaces are different papers and planning phase. Paper is made by putting different stringy materials through novel processing, handling, refining and completing strategies. The surface of the surface, tooth, gnaws off the dry media as it is dragged over the surface.

2. Paper utilized for drawings may be smooth or unpleasant textured (toothed). A decent drawing paper with an unpleasant surface chomps and holds graphite better. A harsh surface will give high complexity to pencil drawings. A firm, smooth completion will bring about low pencil contrast. Make ink drawings on smooth, firm-completed paper or cardstock. Apply washes to a thick, permeable water shading paper surface. Be mindful so as not to apply an excess of wash or the paper will clasp.

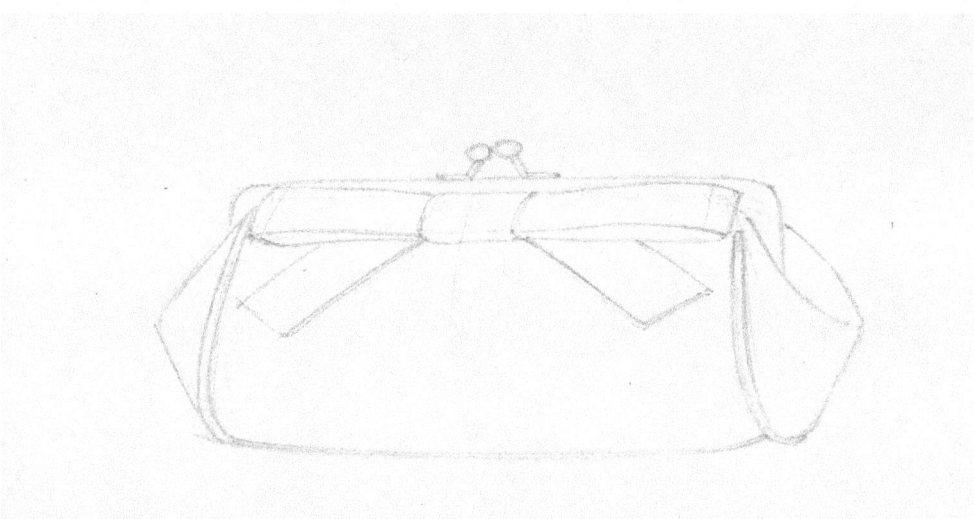

3. Papers are measured in rate of cloth substance and acridity/alkylin adjusting.

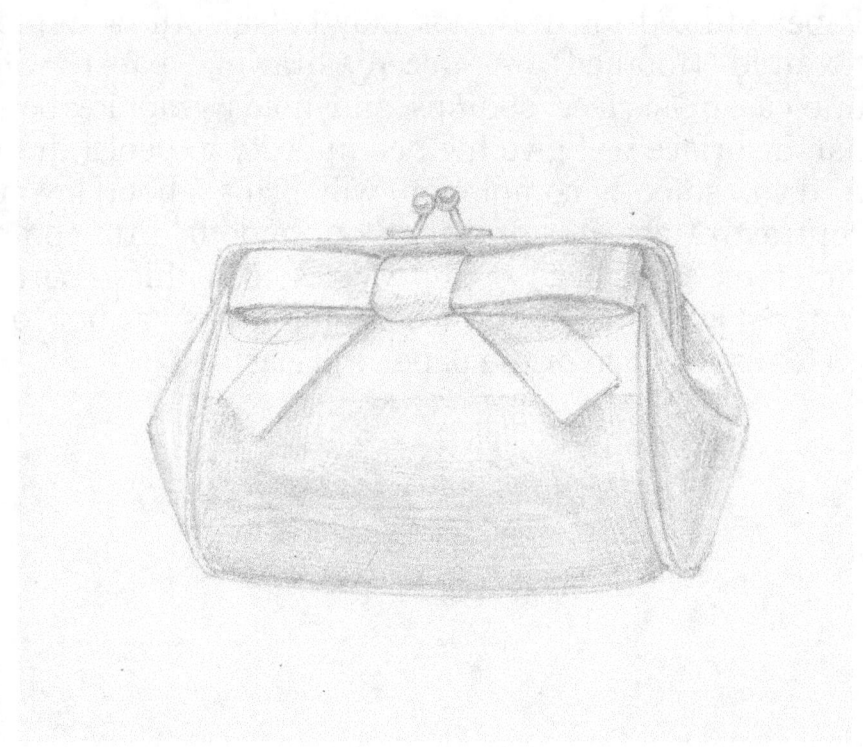

Sketching of an apple

Step 1. Start by outlining a square and separation it daintily down the middle. We will utilize polygon shapes to frame the apple rather than a circle, this will make a more one of a kind looking apple.

Step 2. Here's the fun part. Utilize the crate as a manual for help you put the lines in the right places. Try not to stress over making any bends yet, that is the following step. Include a leaf and a calculated line for the stem on top.

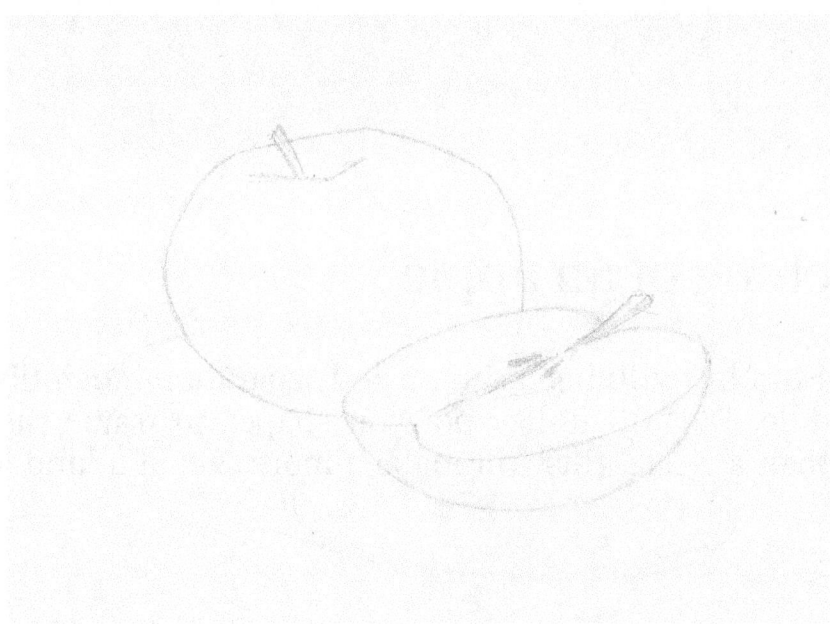

Not all apples are the same, so it's OK if your apple doesn't look precisely like this one. A few apples are extremely round, some have a remarkable shape like this one. Notice there are 3 little knocks on the base of the apple. The highest point of the apple has a wide M shape.

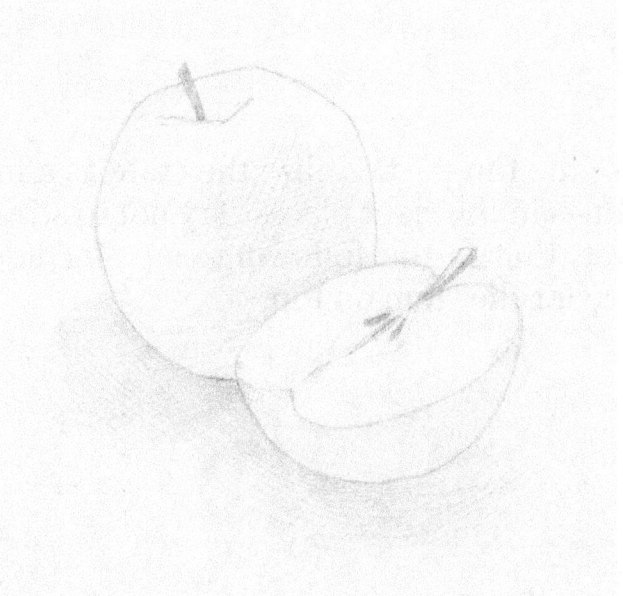

Step 3. Presently you can bend those sharp points. Smooth out only the sharp corners, however keep alternate parts of the lines the same. The apple will come to fruition. Delicately eradicate the past portrayal lines from the last step. Sketch in the shadow under the apple to make a surface for the apple to remain on.

Point of interest the leaf with 4 to 5 veins on every side, and thicken the stem. Notice that the highest point of the apple's stem flares out a bit, and you can see the top edge of the stem as well.

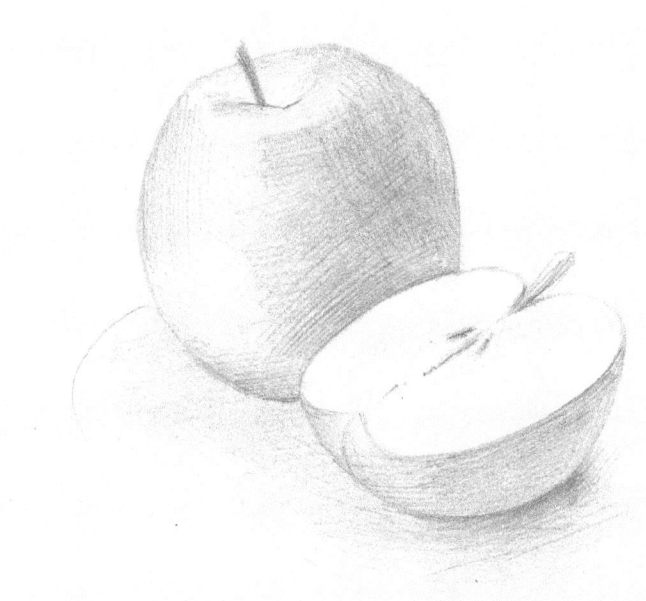

Step 4. Shading. Take as much time as necessary and dependably begin with light strokes when you shade, utilization cross-bring forth strokes. For this lesson we will just shade the internal edge of the apple, the leaf, and shade under the apple. The leaf gets heavier measurements of shading on one side, and light on the other to make a slight fold. Obscure the stem yet not the highest point of the stem. It's OK to utilize your eraser on the off chance that you over-obscured a few ranges while shading.

Steps for Sketching heels

Step 1.

Delicately outline a wedge. Contingent upon how high you need the heel to be, expand or reduction the tallness of the wedge.

Step 2.

Daintily portray in a foot laying on the wedge you beforehand drew. The foot will serve as the aide for high heel.

Step 3.

Daintily draw how you need the shoe to check out the foot, and choose on the off chance that you need to utilize particular plans.

Step 4.

Consistently portray in the real shoe, and recall to eradicate lines and bends that are no more required.

Step 5.

You may utilize a calligraphy pen to draw the framework of your shoe's official shape. Delete overabundance lines when required.

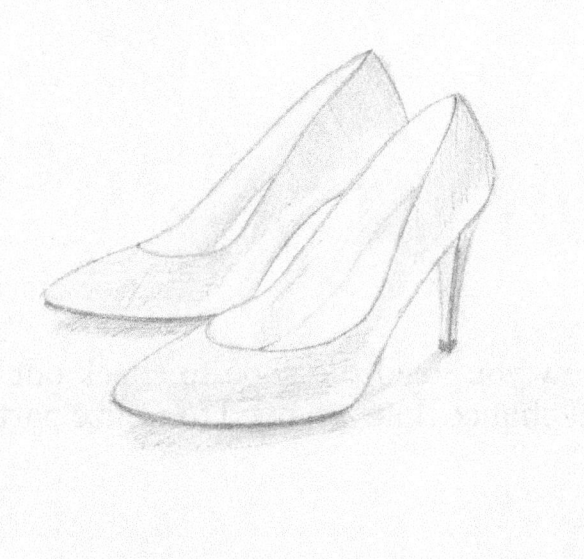

Step 6.

Delete and evacuate whatever remains of the portrayal imprints if not done as of now.

Step 7.

Begin with coloring.

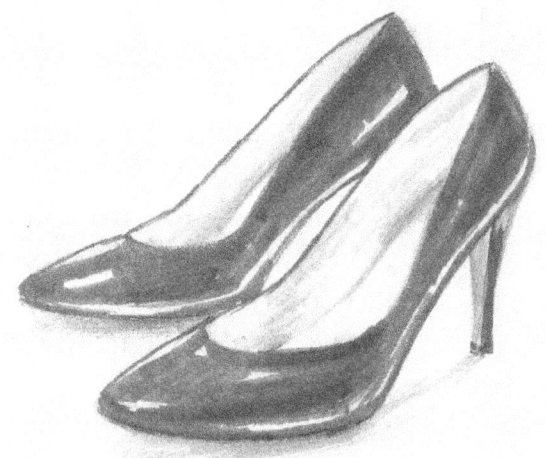

Steps on Sketching

Sketching is the act of drawing an unpleasant diagram or unfinished copy variant of a last bit of workmanship. Sketching can be utilized as a part of readiness for an expansive bit of workmanship, or to simply get a thought of how something will look. Whether you're sketching for the sake of entertainment or for a venture, taking in the correct strategy can make the practice a great deal more agreeable.

Get the right materials. Much the same as with any fine art, it is hard to outline when utilizing low quality (or the wrong) materials. You can without much of a stretch discover all the best possible sketching materials at a neighborhood expressions and artworks store. Spend a couple of dollars and get together all the right materials, including:

H pencils. H pencils are the hardest pencils, and are utilized for sketching slim, straight, non-mix capable lines. These are basically utilized for building design and business outlines. Get a grouping including 6H, 4H, and 2H pencils (6 is the hardest, 2 is the mildest).

B pencils. B pencils are the gentlest pencils, and are utilized for making smeared and foggy lines and for shading your portrayal. These are the top picks of numerous craftsmen. Get a combination including 6B, 4B, and 2B (6B is the gentlest, 2B is the hardest).

Compelling artwork paper. Sketching on customary printer paper may be simple, however the paper is thin and doesn't hold the pencil too. Utilize artistic work paper with a touch of composition for the most effortless time sketching, and for the best general appearance.

Pick you're subject. For amateurs, it is most straightforward to portray from a live model or a picture, instead of by utilizing your creative ability to make a picture to draw. Discover a picture of something you like, or search for an item or individual around you to draw. Take a few minutes to examine the subject before starting to outline. Pay consideration on these things:

Discover the wellspring of light. Finding the essential light source will figure out where you outline the lightest and where you draw the darkest.

Search for any development. Whether genuine development from a genuine subject or saw development in a picture, deciding development in your subject will focus the shape/bearing you make your portrayal strokes.

Pay consideration on essential shapes. All articles are comprised of a mix of the essential shapes (square, circle, triangle, and so forth.). Search for the shapes that underlay you're subject, and portrayal these first.

Try not to draw too vigorously. A portrayal is expected to the base or draft of a picture. In this way, when you begin your representation you ought to utilize a light hand and bunches of short, snappy strokes. This will make it simpler to test out distinctive methods for drawing a specific question, and will permit you to delete botches much less demanding too.

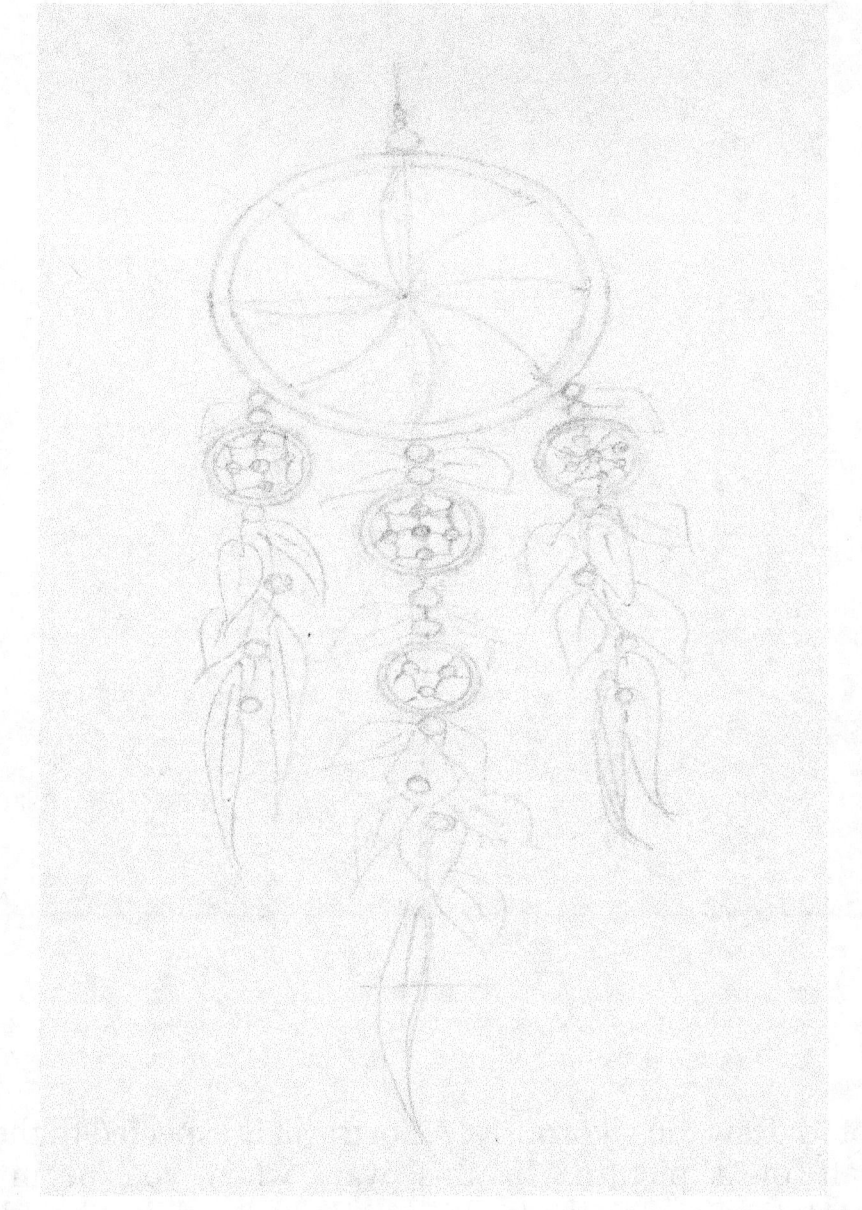

Have a go at doing a signal drawing. Motion drawing is a type of sketching where you utilize constant developments and associated lines to draw you're subject, while never taking a gander at your paper. In spite of the fact that it sounds troublesome, it can help you to get a smart thought of the essential structures in you is drawing, and help to set a base for your last drawing. To do a signal drawing, take a gander at your subject and move your hand appropriately on the paper. At the point when conceivable, abstain from lifting your pencil and utilization covering lines. Later, you can backpedal and eradicate the additional lines and flawless your representation.

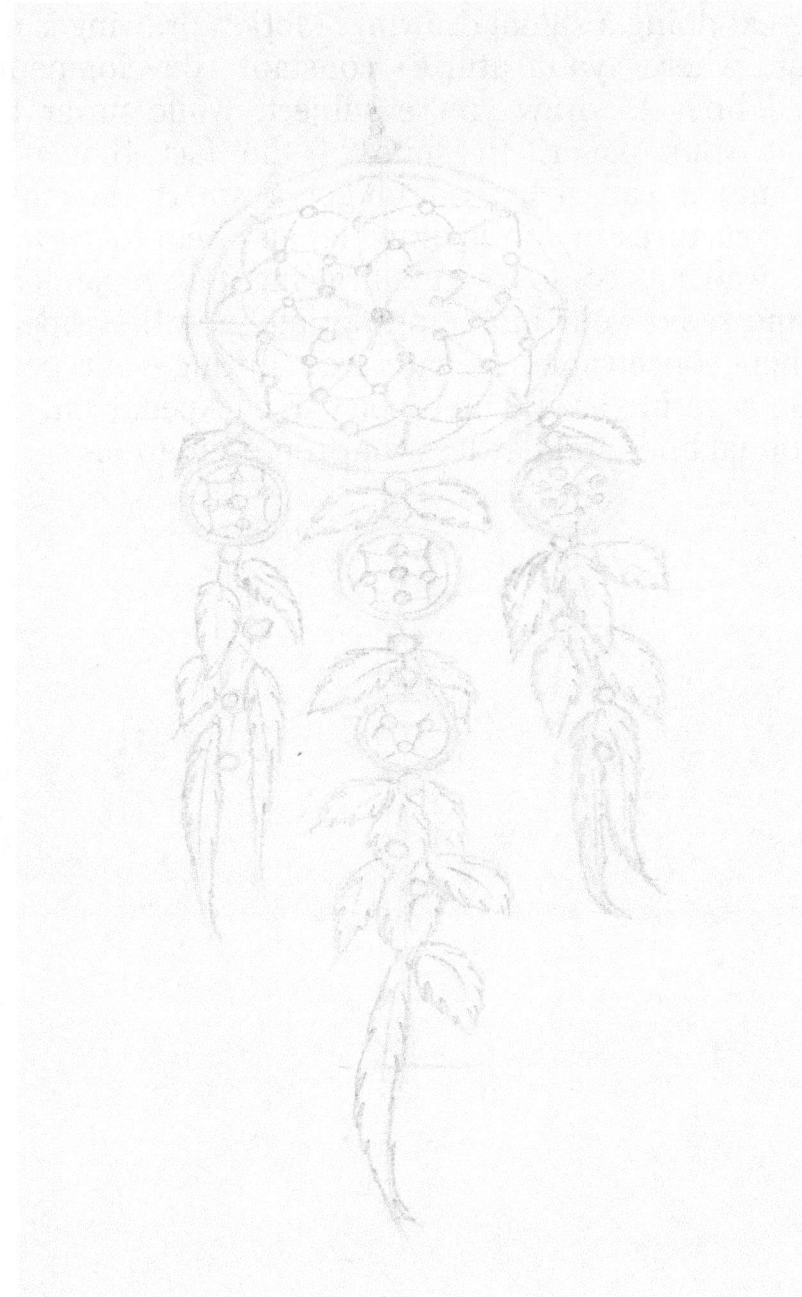

This is great practice for a representation - sort of like a pre-sketch.

Assemble all materials recorded. Verify you have enough light. You can outline at a table, in the recreation center, amidst the city in a sketchbook, on general paper, or even on a napkin.

You may need to attempt diverse renditions of the same article to conceptualize and later choose which you like best.

Before you begin sketching, practice some hand developments. For instance, you can draw circles or level lines for five-ten minutes to warm up your hand.

Beginning with your H pencil, utilize light strokes with free hands. Move your hand rapidly, utilizing negligible weight, verging on sparkling over the page without halting. Get settled with the paper you are working with. At this beginning stage, you ought to scarcely have the capacity to see the strokes. Consider this to be the establishment of your representation.

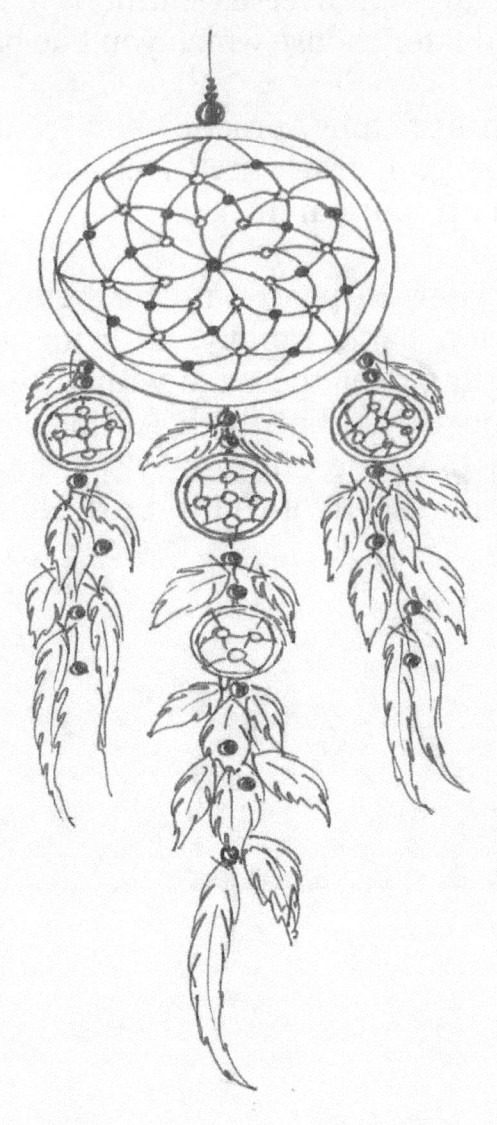

For the following stage, utilize the darker 6 B pencil. When you accomplish the ideal shape in Step 3, you can then characterize your strokes all the more absolutely with this darker pencil. Continue including points of interest. Begin including internal shapes. Verify they are proportional. Case in point, when drawing a stopping slope, you need to verify that the passages and parking spaces are the suitable size.

When you are done utilizing this pencil, you will notice smears on the pages following the lead on this pencil is gentler than the past one. Evacuate all smears with the eraser.

Verify you utilize a delicate eraser like the putty eraser so that your deleting does not sham the top layer of the page. The putty eraser will help your lines, not totally kill them.

How to sketch a candle

Figuring out how to draw light is about difference—and one of the most ideal approaches to practice is by drawing a candle and a flame. In this aide, you'll find out about the shapes and edges connected with light: the faltering teardrop state of the flame and its smooth, gleaming edges; the roasted wick; the liquid rivulets of wax; and the dissolving state of the candle.

Step 1

Draw the dissolved top of the candle and the sides. Incorporate some trickle dots on the left side. Draw the candle around 5 creeps (12.75cm) tall.

Around 3 creeps (7.75cm) from the top, draw the curved top of the candlestick. Begin this by drawing a weak, level line that develops past the candle the same sum on both sides. At that point draw the circular bend of the opening took after by the edge. Draw both parts of the edge circle to precisely make the retreating edge bend that vanishes behind the candle. Draw the vertical bends of the candlestick to mirror one another.

Step 3

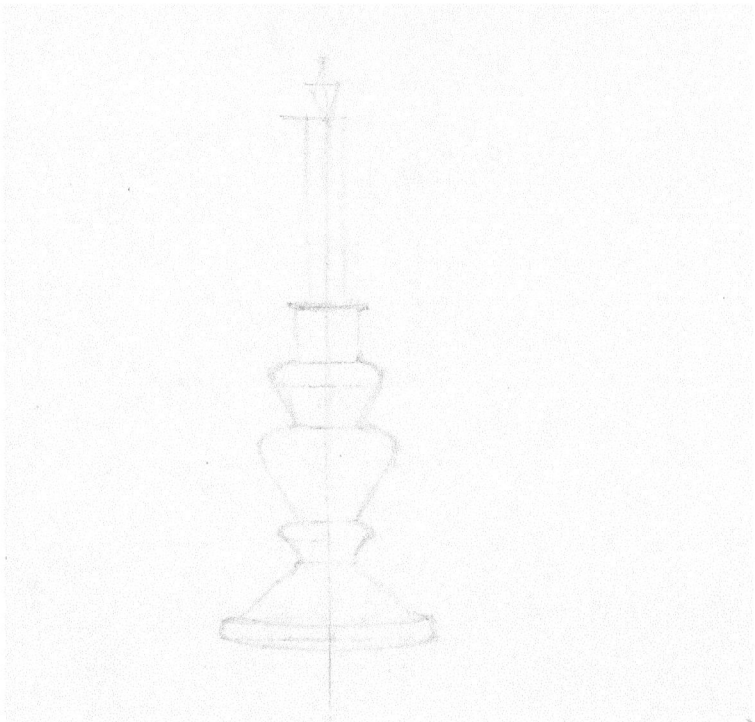

Draw the twisted wick with even thickness. Draw the bend of the closer edge of the highest point of the candle. Include the shapes of the bending liquid wax running down the side of the candle. It points out marginally at the edge and bends back in as it streams down the candlestick. Obscure the line of the candlestick opening along the edges.

Step 4

Shade the whole foundation with delicate vertical imprints. Make notwithstanding shading with the side of the pencil tip. Pivot the pencil a quarter turn clockwise every 5 to 10 strokes, then hone it.

Step 5

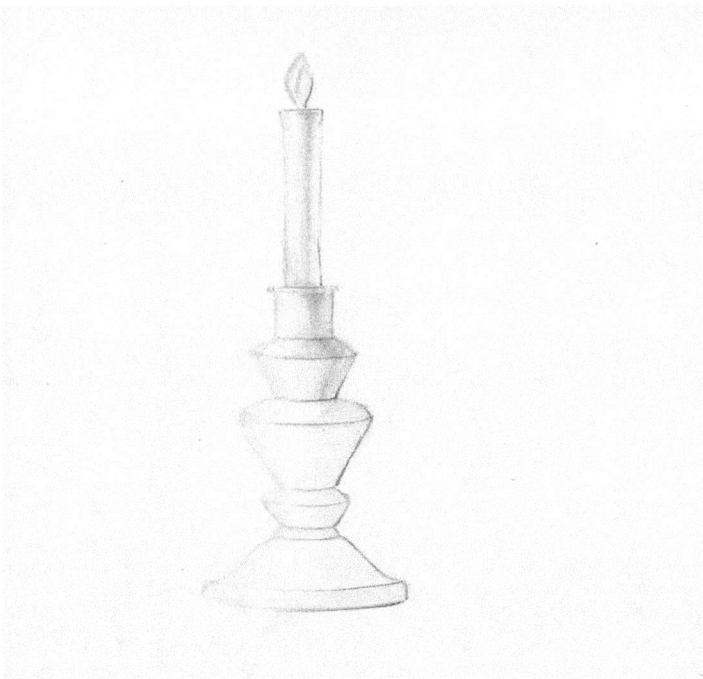

Shade the whole foundation again with strokes that point 45 degrees to one side, then one more layer at 45 degrees to one side. Add to a beat and work on keeping up predictable weight as you make even layers.

Step 6

Shade the candle with a degree that is light at the top and darker at the base. Shade the liquefied wax independently to be lighter, with darker shading along the edge to make the dream of adjusting. Obscure the shading in the more tightly hole.

Step 7

Shade underneath the candlestick edge around the wax trickles in an unpredictable degree that is light under the edge and darker as it continues descending while it gets to be lighter along the side, as well. Shade the wax dribbles darker in the middle and lighter along the edges.

Step 8

Shade the highest point of the candlestick with level strokes and make the fantasy of a cast shadow by shading darker toward the candle. Shade the edge's slim vertical edge dull in the middle and lighter along the edges.

Step 9

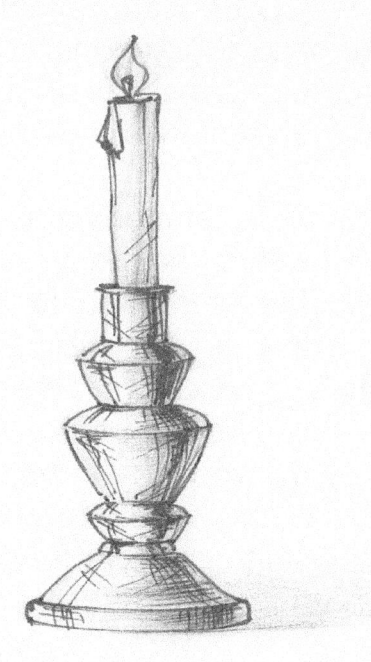

Shade the wick darker at the base of the flame and lighter in the inside.
Propelled Variation

Obscure the estimation of the foundation to heighten the impact of the flame's light. Shade it to show variety from dim to extremely dull close to the flame to make more noteworthy enthusiasm there.

Since you know how to draw a candle and flame, you can work on sketching other light sources. Glad drawing.

Sketching is similar to a sea, you will never at any point get done with realizing, how much ever you learn. There are heaps of things staying to learn in the realm of craftsmanship. The primary motivation behind sketching is to get the stream of your feelings on paper as a picture. Representations are generally finished in two stages, one is preparatory stage and the other one is the last stage. It helps a craftsman to demonstrate his focusing so as to draw capacity on distinctive parts of a specific subject. You can utilize numerous things as a drawing medium, for example, a pen, pencil, watercolors, mud, and so forth.

Sketching is an exceptionally smooth and simple procedure; it additionally gives a brilliant chance to a craftsman where he can deal with diverse thoughts before he makes a last outline of representations. While making a representation, craftsman can feel casual as he doesn't need to make a big deal about committing errors. You can read numerous books accessible in the business sector which give will you brief thoughts regarding how to draw. There are numerous instructional meetings sorted out by acclaimed specialists to give legitimate learning about how to draw. One ought to remember numerous fundamental things which are exceptionally important to while dealing with a portrayal. Some of them are an ink pen, paper, pencil, eraser, and so forth. The craftsman ought to concentrate on the article to make its portrayal legitimately.

Verify that the craftsman does not make utilization of dim strokes while making a portrayal. Additionally he ought not utilize an eraser all the time. Shading is likewise an essential piece of sketching; so it is extremely fundamental that the craftsman keeps this point in his brain while making a portrayal. On the off chance that anybody might want to know the precise rules about how to portray then he ought to concentrate on the sketchbooks of Leonardo da Vinci and Edgar Degas.

Is it accurate to say that you are ready to convey your inventiveness on to your canvas? Will you make a move regulated, on the off chance that I help you to learn drawings and artistic creations until you succeed? Snatch 6 lessons on Oil, Acrylic, Watercolor, Fabric Painting, Pencil Drawing, Color Theory.

It is pivotal never to think about how a hand ought to resemble. Likewise the finest craftsmen take a gander at the hand they are not utilizing before them as an illustration when they are drafting hands. In like manner you ought to discover a pocket-sized reflect and utilization it to take a gander at your hand from alternate points of view or to change your left hand into a right hand.

A repeating beginner's issue is to make the hands excessively little. You ought to look at the extents precisely when you draw a hand. As a rule, position your hand before your head. Watch how it goes the distance from the button to your hairline. Think about this particularly when sketching hands on or close to individuals' heads in your drawings.

Whilst beginning to mull over how to draw hands it is perfect to portray an unstrained hand act first. Notice how the digits are not level when the hand is unstrained. They the majority of the time twist a bit, the little finger a great deal more than the forefinger.

In the first place break down the extents of your digits. Take a gander at your digits with the palm dismissed. You will find that the digits are pretty nearly one-a large portion of the length of the complete hand. Each finger is separated into three segments of distinctive lengths. The upper segment (with the nail) is around 66% of the center part, and the inside part is around 66% of the lower part (which offers path to the knuckles).

Presently for a tad bit enchantment! Turn your hand all over so you see it from the palm side. The extents of the digits have changed now clearly! The digits now look much shorter. In the event that you measure them you will find they are a great deal under one-a large portion of the length of the hand. The reason: the skin between the digits shows up as a feature of the palm.

Notwithstanding this watch that every one of the three components of the digits now are all of about equivalent length. At the point when sketching hands it's vital to recall this so you don't fall into the trap of sketching indistinguishable digits regardless of which way you take a gander at them.

The thumb is an altogether diverse thing, so don't draw it as some other finger. It just has two joints, not three, goes in an alternate bearing and has a totally diverse frame so see it with consideration. You should likewise see how it twists daintily when completely broadened.

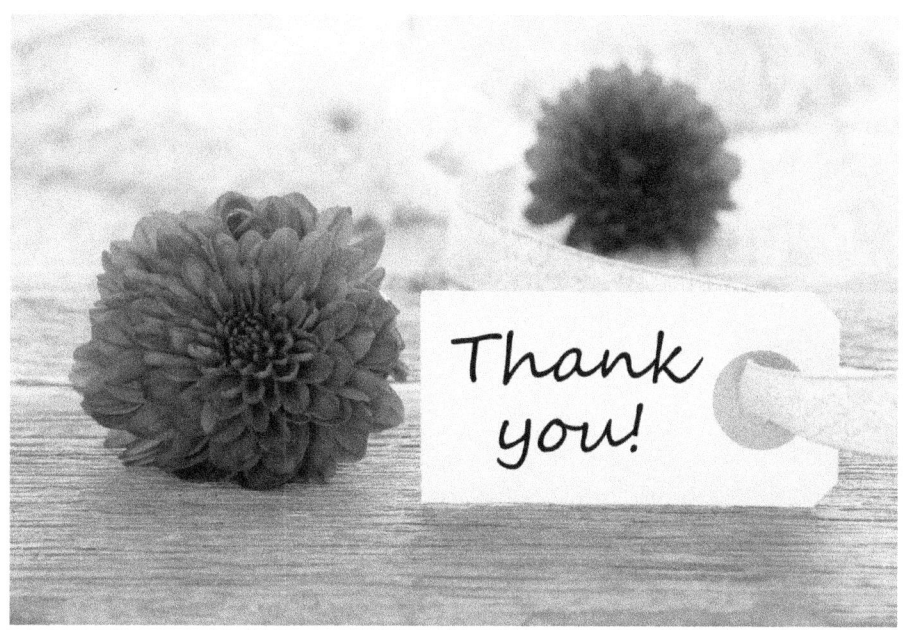

Finally, if you enjoyed this book, then I'd like to ask you for a favor, would you be kind enough to leave a review for this book on Amazon? It'd be greatly appreciated!

Click here to leave a review for this book on Amazon!

Thank you and good luck!

www.ingramcontent.com/pod-product-compliance
Lightning Source LLC
Chambersburg PA
CBHW080609190526
45169CB00007B/2948